Serving Your Country

The Blue Angels:

The U.S. Navy Flight Demonstration Squadron

by Glen and Karen Bledsoe

CAPSTONE
HIGH-INTEREST
BOOKS

an imprint of Capstone Press
Mankato, Minnesota

Capstone High-Interest Books are published by Capstone Press
151 Good Counsel Drive, P.O. Box 669, Mankato, Minnesota 56002
http://www.capstone-press.com

Library of Congress Cataloging-in-Publication Data
Bledsoe, Glen.
    The Blue Angels: The U.S. Navy Flight Demonstration Squadron/by Glen and
Karen Bledsoe.
        p. cm.—(Serving your country)
        Includes bibliographical references (p. 45) and index.
        ISBN 0-7368-0773-X
        1. United States. Naval Flight Demonstration Squadron—Juvenile literature.
[1. United States. Naval Flight Demonstration Squadron. 2. Aeronautics, Military.
3. Stunt flying.] I. Bledsoe, Karen E. II. Title. III. Series.
VG94.6.N38 B58 2001
797.5'4'0973—dc21   00-009821

Summary: Describes the U.S. Navy's Blue Angels, their history, aircraft, maneuvers,
and team members.

Editorial Credits
Carrie A. Braulick, editor; Lois Wallentine, product planning editor;
    Timothy Halldin, cover designer; Linda Clavel, production designer
    and illustrator; Katy Kudela, photo researcher

Photo Credits
Bob Schillereff, cover, 4, 37, 38, 40
David O. Bailey, 20, 23, 32, 35
National Museum of Naval Aviation, 10, 13, 15, 17
Unicorn Stock Photos/Russell R. Grundke, 6; Dennis Thompson, 18;
    Terry Barner, 29, 43; Aneal Vohra, 30

**Special thanks to the Blue Angel Public Affairs Office staff for their assistance
in preparing this book.**

1 2 3 4 5 6 06 05 04 03 02 01

Table of Contents

Chapter 1

The Blue Angels

The six pilots take off from the runway in their planes. The audience at the air show watches these pilots perform daring maneuvers and stunts. The pilots roll, dive, and fly upside down. They sometimes fly as one unit. At other times, two pilots perform maneuvers separate from the other planes. A group of U.S. military pilots flies the planes. This group is called the Blue Angels.

Navy and Marine Corps Representatives

The Blue Angels represent the U.S. Navy and the U.S. Marine Corps. Military leaders hope that the Blue Angels will inspire people to consider a career in these groups.

The Blue Angels perform maneuvers with six planes.

The Blue Angels fly blue and gold F/A-18 Hornets.

The Blue Angels perform in about 70 air shows each show season. Their show season runs from March through November. The Blue Angels perform at about 35 locations during these months.

The Blue Angels often perform at air shows throughout the United States. They sometimes fly in Canada, Japan, and European countries. In 1992, the Blue Angels became the first flight demonstration team to perform in Russia.

Blue Angels' Shows

Blue Angels' shows last about 45 minutes. Six pilots perform during these shows. The pilots usually perform about 30 different maneuvers during each show. They leave only 15 seconds between maneuvers.

The Blue Angels often fly together in formation. The main Blue Angel formation is called the Delta. All six pilots form a triangle shape in this formation.

Two pilots sometimes perform maneuvers separate from the formations. These pilots are called solos. The solos and the pilots in formation take turns performing during shows.

The narrator also takes part in shows. This Blue Angel describes the pilots' maneuvers to the audience. The narrator also takes reporters for rides at each show.

Blue Angels' Emblem

The Blue Angels fly F/A-18 Hornets. These planes are both fighter and attack planes. Fighter planes are designed to shoot down enemy planes. Attack planes are designed to hit ground targets. The F/A-18s are painted blue with gold trim. Blue and gold are the Navy's official colors.

Chapter 2
Blue Angels' History

The Navy had flight demonstration teams before the Blue Angels. In 1927, the Navy organized the Three Sea Hawks. This three-pilot demonstration team flew until September 1928. The High Hatters of VF-1B flew from 1929 until the early 1930s.

The Marine Corps also formed a flight demonstration team. This team flew during the early 1930s. But flight demonstration teams disbanded when World War II (1939–1945) began. The U.S. military needed its pilots to perform combat duties.

Roy Voris formed the Blue Angels in 1946.

The Blue Angels Form

By 1946, many of the military members who had served during World War II had left the military. At the time, James Forrestal was Secretary of the Navy. Chester Nimitz was Chief of Naval Operations. The two men wanted to inspire people to join the Navy by forming a flight demonstration team. Forrestal and Nimitz sent a message about their idea to officials at the Naval Air Advanced Training Command in Pensacola, Florida. Many Navy pilots train at this naval air station (NAS). Commander Hugh Winters received the message. Winters asked Lieutenant Commander Roy Voris if he would like to organize the demonstration team.

Voris agreed and began to form the team in April. The team's name became The Flight Exhibition Team.

Voris chose Grumman F-6F Hellcat fighter planes for the team. The F-6Fs had large propellers. These rotating metal blades provide force to move planes through the air. Voris hired a painter to paint the planes blue and gold.

Grumman F-6F Hellcats had large propellers.

Voris chose three pilots to perform with him. These pilots were Lieutenants Mel Cassidy, Maurice Wickendoll, and L.G. Barnard. But Barnard was assigned to another unit. Lieutenant Gale Stouse replaced him. All of the pilots were unmarried. Voris thought that unmarried men would be more committed to flying.

Three of the team's pilots flew in formation. This formation was made up of a flight leader, a right wing, and a left wing. Voris was the flight leader. He also was called "boss." Voris flew ahead of the other two pilots. Wickendoll was the right wing. He flew on Voris's right side. Cassidy was the left wing. He flew on Voris's left side.

Stouse flew a fighter plane called a North American SNJ Texan. This plane was painted to look like a Japanese fighter plane called the A6M Zero. The Japanese Zero was successful against U.S. aircraft during World War II. The other pilots pretended to shoot this plane down during their performances.

Voris also chose 11 men for his ground crew. The ground crew maintained and repaired the team's planes.

First Performances

Voris and his team practiced for several weeks. At the time, Commander Dan Smith was director of training for the Air Advanced Training Command in Pensacola. On May 10, the team performed for Smith.

Voris was the Blue Angels' first flight leader.

Two days later, the team performed for Rear Admiral Ralph Davidson at NAS Jacksonville in Florida. Admirals are the highest ranking naval officers. Davidson then asked the team to perform for Vice Admiral Frank Wagner.

The team's performance for Wagner was not perfect. Stouse threw out a sawdust-filled dummy when other team members pretended to shoot his plane down. The dummy was attached to a parachute. But the parachute did not open. The dummy hit the ground only a short distance from Wagner. Sawdust flew into the air.

However, Wagner still liked the show. He told Forrestal that the team was ready to perform for the public. The team performed its first show for the public on June 15 in Jacksonville.

A New Name

The Flight Exhibition Team members wanted to have a more interesting name. Voris started a contest to name the team. Navy members sent in many suggestions. Navy Chief of Staff Bill Gentner liked the name Blue Lancers. But Voris did not like this name.

Cassidy, Voris, and Wickendoll flew in formation during their first performances.

A few days later, Wickendoll was looking at a *New Yorker* magazine. He saw an advertisement for the Blue Angel Nightclub in the magazine. He thought Blue Angels was a good name for the demonstration team. Wickendoll suggested the name to Voris. Voris also liked the name.

The team then performed in Omaha, Nebraska. Voris told reporters there how he liked the name Blue Angels. The reporters used the

The Blue Angels began to fly F8F-1 Bearcats in August 1946.

name in their newspaper articles. Others then began to use the name for the team. It became the team's official name.

New Planes

In August 1946, the Blue Angels began to use a different type of propeller plane. They flew Grumman F8F-1 Bearcats. The team preferred

Bearcats because they were more powerful and easier to handle than Hellcats.

In August 1949, the Blue Angels started to use Grumman F9F-2 Panthers. These planes had jet engines. Planes with jet engines burn fuel to create exhaust gases. The exhaust gases rush out the rear of the planes. This action causes the planes to move forward. Previous Blue Angel planes had engines with pistons. These circular metal pieces move up and down to create power for planes. Planes with jet engines are much more powerful than planes with piston engines.

Over the years, the Blue Angels have flown other jet engine planes. They flew Grumman F9F-8 Cougars from 1953 to 1956. They flew Grumman F11F-1 Tigers from 1957 to 1968. The pilots then flew McDonnell Douglas F-4J Phantoms through the 1973 show season. In 1974, the Blue Angels began flying McDonnell Douglas A-4F Skyhawks. They continued to fly Skyhawks through the 1985 show season. The team began flying F/A-18 Hornets in November 1986.

Chapter 3
Aircraft and Maneuvers

The Blue Angels plan and practice many maneuvers for their shows. They never repeat a maneuver during a show The Blue Angels' F/A-18s have features to help the pilots perform their maneuvers.

The F/A-18 Hornet
The F/A-18 Hornet is 56 feet (17 meters) long and 15.4 feet (4.7 meters) tall. The F/A-18's wingspan is 37.5 feet (11.4 meters) long. Wingspan is the distance between the tips of an airplane's wings.

The Blue Angels perform various maneuvers during air shows.

F/A-18s fly slower than many other fighter planes. Their top speed is 1,200 miles (1,931 kilometers) per hour. Some fighter planes can fly 1,875 miles (3,017 kilometers) per hour. But maneuvers are easier to perform at slower speeds. The Blue Angels usually fly about 350 miles (560 kilometers) per hour during shows.

Blue Angel F/A-18s do not carry weapons. Pilots only fly these planes for demonstrations. But the planes can be equipped with weapons and ready for combat in about three days.

Supply Plane

The Blue Angels also use a Lockheed Martin C-130 Hercules plane. This large plane carries supplies and Blue Angel support personnel to air shows. The plane is called "Fat Albert." The Blue Angels began using Fat Albert in 1970.

Eight Marine Corps members make up Fat Albert's crew. Three of these Marines are pilots. These pilots must have 1,200 hours of flight experience. Two flight engineers, a navigator, a flight mechanic, and a loadmaster also are on the crew. The flight engineers are the senior enlisted

Fat Albert carries supplies and support personnel to air shows.

flight crewmembers. The navigator is responsible for all flight planning and navigation. This crewmember makes sure the plane travels on course. The flight mechanic maintains and repairs the plane. The loadmaster makes sure all necessary equipment and support personnel are on the aircraft.

Delta Formation

Each plane has its own place and number in the Delta formation. The boss flies plane No. 1. This plane leads the other planes in the formation.

The right wing flies plane No. 2. This pilot flies behind and to the right of plane No. 1. A Marine Corps pilot usually flies this plane. Navy members fly in the other planes. The left wing flies plane No. 3. This pilot flies behind and to the left of plane No.1. The slot pilot flies plane No. 4. This pilot flies behind and to the inside of planes No. 2 and No. 3.

Solo pilots fly planes No. 5 and No. 6. The pilot of plane No. 5 is called the lead solo. The pilot of plane No. 6 is called the opposing solo. These pilots fly behind and to the outside of the wing pilots.

Formation Maneuvers

The Blue Angels fly basic Navy and Marine Corps maneuvers. But the Blue Angels perform them faster, closer together, and closer to the ground.

The Delta

Blue Angel #1	Flight leader
Blue Angel #2	Right wing
Blue Angel #3	Left wing
Blue Angel #4	Slot
Blue Angel #5	Lead solo
Blue Angel #6	Opposing solo

Blue Angels perform some maneuvers in the Delta formation. They may do the Delta Roll. In this maneuver, pilots roll over sideways in a complete circle.

Another maneuver is the Loop Break Cross. The pilots first fly straight up in the Delta formation. They make a loop. They reach the top of the loop at about 8,000 feet (2,400 meters). All six planes fly in different directions as they complete the loop and fly downward. The planes then fly upward, approach each other, and cross paths.

The Diamond Roll is another maneuver. Four planes fly in the Diamond formation. The wingtips of the boss's plane are only 36 inches (91 centimeters) above the canopies of the left and right wing planes. A canopy covers an airplane's cockpit. The slot pilot's canopy is 36 inches (91 centimeters) under the wingtips of the wing planes.

The Blue Angels also use the Diamond formation during the Farvel maneuver. But the boss flies upside down. In the Double Farvel, both the boss and slot pilot fly upside down.

Blue Angel Formations

Echelon

Line Abreast

Double Farvel

Diamond

 Inverted planes

In the Echelon Pass, the boss, right and left wings, and slot pilots line up diagonally. The nose of each plane is next to the wings of the plane in front of it.

One of the most difficult maneuvers is the Line Abreast Loop. During this maneuver, five planes line up side by side. They complete a loop as they remain in line.

Solo Maneuvers

Solos may perform after the formation maneuvers. The formation pilots regroup while the solos perform. Solos often fly faster than pilots in formation.

The lead solo may perform the Dirty Roll soon after take off. This pilot rolls over sideways with the plane's landing gear down.

In the Knife-edge Pass, the two solos fly toward one another at high speeds. They tilt to fly sideways as they pass each other.

Another solo maneuver is the Double Tuckover Roll. Both solos fly upside down. The planes are 150 feet (46 meters) above the

The Blue Angels sometimes fly in the Echelon formation.

ground. The planes roll sideways as they pass each other.

During the Sneak, four planes fly in the Diamond formation. They fly low in front of the audience. The opposing solo then flies above the audience after sneaking up from behind them. The lead solo flies above the audience from the left. This maneuver is meant to surprise the audience.

Chapter 4

The Blue Angel Team

The Blue Angel team includes 16 officers and about 100 support personnel. Officers hold higher ranks than enlisted personnel. They have more education and training than enlisted personnel. The officers include the six demonstration pilots, narrator, events coordinator, and three Marine Corps C-130 pilots. The events coordinator schedules the air shows and organizes travel plans. Five support personnel members also are Blue Angel officers.

Blue Angel support personnel may work in one of several areas. These areas include maintenance, supply, public affairs, and administration. Personnel also may work in the

The Blue Angel team is made up of 16 officers and about 100 support personnel.

Navy and Marine Corps members who want to become pilots must meet various qualifications.

events coordinator's office, on the C-130 flight crew, or on the medical crew. All Navy and Marine Corps members volunteer for their Blue Angel positions. About 50 Blue Angel team members travel to each show.

The Blue Angels are based at NAS Pensacola in Florida. Blue Angel team members live there when they are not performing official duties.

Blue Angel Pilots

Naval and Marine Corps commanding officers recommend pilots for the Blue Angels. The current Blue Angel pilots choose new pilots. Each pilot serves on the team for two years. About three new pilots join the team each year. All current pilots must agree on each choice.

Blue Angel pilots must meet certain qualifications. They must be career officers. Career officers are people who plan to serve in the military for many years. They also must have at least 1,350 hours of fighter or attack plane experience.

All pilot candidates must be carrier qualified. These pilots can land their planes on an aircraft carrier. These large warships have a flight deck where airplanes can take off and land.

Most pilots chosen for the team have flown at least 10 years. Many of these pilots also have been flight instructors.

Candidates for the Blue Angels' boss must have 3,000 fighter or attack plane flight hours of experience. These candidates also must have commanded a fighter or attack plane unit. The Chief of Naval Air Training chooses the boss.

Support Personnel

Commanding officers recommend support personnel for the team. These personnel have demonstrated excellent performance in their specialized areas. Current members of the Blue Angels' support team then choose the new personnel.

Many support personnel are maintenance crewmembers. They maintain and repair the F/A-18s. The maintenance crew works on the planes at least two hours before a show. They check each plane's equipment. They also may work after the pilots finish flying.

Other support personnel work in other areas. The supply team makes sure the pilots have the necessary supplies at air shows. For example, they make sure enough spare airplane parts are available. Members of the public affairs department make show places and times available to the public. They also answer

The maintenance crew makes sure the Blue Angels' F/A-18s are operating properly.

questions about the Blue Angels. Personnel in the events coordinator's office make hotel reservations and other travel plans for the team.

The medical crew makes sure all Blue Angel team members receive proper medical care. They also help make sure the team members are healthy.

Most Blue Angel personnel serve on the Blue Angel team for about three years. The maintenance officer, events coordinator, and flight surgeon serve on the team for two years. The maintenance officer is in charge of the maintenance crew. The flight surgeon runs the medical crew.

Pilot Training

During winter, Blue Angel pilots train at the naval air facility in El Centro, California. The Blue Angel pilots begin their training by performing simple routines. They practice maneuvers with a great deal of distance between the planes. As they improve, the pilots decrease the space between the planes.

The pilots also fly slowly and perform maneuvers at high altitudes early in the training season. They fly faster and at lower altitudes as they gain experience.

During training season, the Blue Angels fly six days each week. They fly twice each day. The maintenance officer and the flight surgeon

The Blue Angels sometimes fly in the Diamond formation.

watch them perform. Each flight is videotaped. The pilots watch the videotapes. They try to spot and correct their mistakes.

Safety
The Blue Angels train to fly safely. A small mistake could cause the planes to crash.

Before each demonstration, the pilots meet to mentally practice the show. The boss talks them through the maneuvers. Other pilots close their eyes to visualize the maneuvers. The Blue Angel pilots also talk about the weather before their shows. For example, they talk about wind conditions. The wind strength and direction can affect how their planes fly.

After each demonstration, the pilots meet to discuss the show. This communication helps them correct problems and improve their performances.

The Blue Angels must be careful as they perform maneuvers close to each other.

Chapter 5
The Future

The Blue Angels will continue to represent the Navy and Marine Corps in the future. But they may make changes in aircraft, personnel, and maneuvers.

New Aircraft
In early 2001, the Navy began using a new plane called the F/A-18 E/F Super Hornet. Super Hornets are larger than F/A-18 Hornets. They can fly farther without needing to refuel. Super Hornets also carry more weapons than F/A-18s.

The Blue Angels may use Super Hornets in the future. But the team probably will fly

The Blue Angels will probably fly F/A-18 Hornets for many more years.

F/A-18s for many more years. These planes are well-suited for demonstration flying.

Women Team Members

Before 1993, women in the armed forces could not serve in combat duty. They could not be Blue Angels because they were not allowed to fly fighter planes. Today, women can be fighter pilots. In the future, a woman may fly with the Blue Angels.

Each year, about 12 women serve on the Blue Angel support personnel team. Some women are administrators or serve on the maintenance crew. Other women are public affairs or supply personnel.

Blue Angels and the Public

Blue Angel pilots do not only fly planes. They visit hospitals, schools, and other countries. They often speak to students. They tell the students about the rewards and challenges of being a Blue Angel pilot. They also try to interest the students in careers in the Navy or Marine Corps.

Blue Angel maneuvers such as the Double Farvel will continue to entertain air show audiences.

The Blue Angels show the skills of the Navy and Marine Corps to many people each year. More than 340 million people have watched them perform. Even more people will continue to enjoy the team's performances in the future.

Words to Know

aerobatics (air-uh-BAT-iks)—skillful or dangerous maneuvers performed by aircraft pilots

aircraft carrier (AIR-kraft KA-ree-ur)—a warship with a large flat deck where aircraft take off and land

canopy (KAN-uh-pee)—the sliding cover over an airplane's cockpit

cockpit (KOK-pit)—the area in the front of a plane where the pilot sits

commander (kuh-MAN-dur)—an officer in the Navy who has a ranking above a lieutenant commander and below a captain

maneuver (muh-NOO-vur)—a planned and controlled movement; pilots perform a series of maneuvers at air shows.

propeller (pruh-PEL-ur)—a set of rotating blades that provides force to move a plane through air

To Learn More

Green, Michael. *The United States Navy.*
Serving Your Country. Mankato, Minn.:
Capstone High-Interest Books, 1998.

Suen, Anastasia. *Air Show.* New York: Henry
Holt, 2001.

Van Steenwyk, Elizabeth. *Air Shows: From
Barnstormers to Blue Angels.* A First Book.
New York: Franklin Watts, 1998.

Useful Addresses

International Council of Air Shows
751 Miller Drive SE
Suite F-4
Leesburg, VA 20175

National Museum of Naval Aviation
1750 Radford Boulevard
Suite C
N.A.S. Pensacola, FL 32508

U.S. Navy Blue Angels Alumni Association
P.O. Box 427
St. Francis, MN 55070

U.S. Navy Flight Demonstration Squadron
390 San Carlos Road
Suite A
Pensacola, FL 32508-5508

Internet Sites

AirShowNetwork.com
http://airshownetwork.com

United States Marine Corps
http://www.usmc.mil

United States Navy
http://www.navy.mil

United States Navy Blue Angels
http://www.blucangels.navy.mil

U.S. Navy Blue Angels Alumni Association
http://www.blueangels.org

Index